HOW TO SURVIVE LAW SCHOOL: YEAR 1

A Practical Guide for the Caribbean Law Student

By Giselle Mills

GOM Press

ISBN: 978-1-7325701-2-2

To my parents, Patrice and Henry,
who helped me survive.

Table of Contents

Chapter 1: Introduction

You may be reading this book for any of the following reasons:

- You are thinking about starting law school;
- You are about to start law school;
- You just started law school;
- You are already in law school, you are 'catching your tail', feeling overwhelmed and searching desperately for motivation and/or assistance in surviving the remainder of your academic year;
- You tried and did not succeed completing the law programme and are reconsidering re-entry;
- You survived law school and are curious to know what I have to say on this topic; and/or
- You know me personally and I asked you very nicely to read this book.

If any of the above reasons apply to you, this book is ideal for you! So keep reading.

Audience

This book is primarily written for current and prospective law students pursing the Legal Education Certificate (L.E.C.) issued by the Caribbean Council of Legal Education. However, the practical advice provided throughout can be very useful for law students at both the undergraduate and postgraduate levels around the world.

Why Study Law?

If you are a current law student, you may have been asked this question over a dozen times by now. You may even be sick of hearing the question and being required to answer it. I say 'required to answer it' because a loud 'steups', eye roll, the evil eye, a hard stare or awkward silence are not the best responses when said question is posed to you by one of your tutors on orientation day.

Please be assured that your successful completion of law school will not free you from it either. If you are fortunate enough to attend a job interview, you will hear this clichéd question again. Be prepared.

So, why study law?

For those of you who have no qualms about the question and have the answer at the tip of your tongue - great. For those who are not as certain, I have provided a list of some of the most common answers to this question.

Reasons for Studying Law:

- Money - let's be real. Most people are aware of how lucrative a law career can be. Sure, you may have an altruistic motive but who enters a profession to be broke? Not me.

- Parental pressure - there are different levels of this. There are the parents who decide your career from birth and dictate your life, the ones want to create/continue a family dynasty of lawyers, and the ones who wish they could have been lawyers, who employ regular guilt-trip tactics on you and live vicariously through you. Thus, your entry into law school.

- Accomplish your dream - Has it always been your burning passion to become a lawyer? Or maybe a judge...

- Power and prestige - Let's face it. Many people who choose to pursue law do so for egotistical reasons and are primarily concerned with the attainment of power over others. Hopefully, this is not you. As for the prestige aspect, there is nothing wrong with wanting to improve your social standing and standard of living, but too many people do so for the purpose of boasting. A certain large peacock comes to mind...

- Make a change - Here we have the altruistic reasons. A fair number of persons choose to study law with the goal of making a positive change in society. Whether they pursue this goal upon the attainment of their degrees is another matter entirely, but it is nevertheless a good reason for joining the legal fraternity.

- Challenge yourself - Some people really love intellectual stimulation. Those who pursue law for this reason are like academic daredevils, who get a high off of intellectual challenges. I am sure you know a few.

- You like the sound of your own voice - The talkative, domineering, arrogant types who must be heard on every topic. You know who you are.

- You could not get in to Medical School - I have a colleague who realised too late that he needed to have studied the Sciences to do medicine (like duh) so he chose Law instead.

- Flipped a coin - Heads law school, tails doubles/roti vendor. Hopefully, you weren't this directionless. But if you were, I am glad that your coin led you to this path.

- Mental instability - Does this need an explanation?

Why Did I Study Law?

Three of the above reasons apply to me: It was my dream, I wanted to make a change, and for the money.

Ever since I was a child, I knew that I wanted to become a lawyer (of course, back then I did not know how torturous the path would be!). In fact, as a child, at one point I even dreamed of being a judge. The big robes and the gavel seemed so cool on Judge Judy. Then as I grew older and I began to see beneath the surface of society, I realised that there were too many disenfranchised and underprivileged persons in the world. I wanted to help improve their lives. And then I matured further and economic realities sank in. Not only did I desire to improve the lives of others, but my bank account balance as well.

The Purpose of this Book

Let's be perfectly frank. Law school is not a walk in the park. It is a lot of hard work and stress. A LOT. As someone who survived the ordeal fairly recently, I know exactly what it entails and what is required to succeed. I did not have a guide book like this when I was in law school and I had to learn many things the hard way and all on my own. But I do not want that to be you. I want to save you the trouble that I went through. Why? Because time is our most valuable asset and I would like to save you some of yours. Plus, I care about you and I want you to succeed.

I initially intended to write this guide while I was in law school but I just did not have enough time. Now that I do, here it is.

Last Words...

If you have just been admitted to law school, congratulations! You have achieved much more academically than the average citizen. Now, prepare yourself mentally for the challenges that will lie ahead. If you are in the midst of it, do not give up. This book is here to help you.

With the right attitude and realistic expectations, you can and will survive law school. I wish you the very best of success in this momentous journey and I hope you find this book useful along the way. Godspeed!

Chapter 2: Preliminaries

Before we get into the meat of this book, there are a few matters that you need to consider. In fact, they should be considered before even deciding on whether you will be attending law school.

Law School vs Undergrad

If you attended the University of the West Indies and attained your L.L.B (Bachelor of Laws) degree, you would have been amply warned about how different law school is from the undergraduate programme. I was amply warned. In fact, I heard so many horror stories from tutors about their unpleasant experiences at law school that it made me reconsider my attendance. My Real Property Law tutor told us point blank that she hated law school with a passion and would never in life repeat the experience. So... yeah... not very good motivation there.

In my second year at university, the law faculty actually held a seminar to introduce us to what life would be like as a law school student. All I heard was "realllll work, pressure, stress, zero social life, no life, blood and tears". Again, no great source of motivation there.

Suffice it to say, when I arrived at the Hugh Wooding Law School, I was expecting the next two years of my life to resemble the fires of hell.

The reality was not very far from my expectations. But it was not as impossible as many others had made it seem. It *is* a tonne of work and the deadlines can be stressful. But overall, it really is not hugely different from the undergraduate programme - just a lot more intense. But fear not. If thousands have endured it and survived, then so can you. Just put in the work required and adopt a positive attitude.

What You Need to Consider

Budget

This of course, is crucial. It is most likely the overriding consideration. Whether or not you can afford to do something is usually the driving factor. Law school in particular is quite costly. Unless you are the lucky recipient of a scholarship or have secured private funding, tuition costs are a significant consideration.

In addition to tuition, the following factors discussed below are necessary additions to your budget, i.e. accommodation, supplies, food, clothing, and transportation costs.

Accommodation - hall vs apartment vs home

This is a very important consideration. Where you live during your stint at law school can be a determining factor in your success. You need to find a place that is most conducive to studying. The usual options for students are halls of residence, apartments or living at home.

Halls of Residence:
I lived on hall for all three of my undergraduate years as well as my two years of law school. And I hated it. I am a naturally reserved person who studies best in solitude; I usually prefer a peaceful and quiet environment. One of the halls I resided on threw parties practically every weekend and my room was right next to the recreation room/party zone. The majority of the residents were immature and loud and could care less for my peace of mind. And let's not even get into sanitation! Suffice it to say, living on that hall was not conducive to my studying nor my blood pressure. I found out shortly after moving on that hall that I was the only law student residing there. I remember several of the residents giving me pitying looks when I told them my area of study.

But do not let my bad experience sway you. I moved to a different hall for my law school years and it was not as bad as the first one. By the time I moved there I had built up a strong immunity to noise and blasting music, so much so that I would sometimes bob my head to the various beats while reflecting. This hall often suffered from water and electricity outages though, but still was not as bad as the first one. I had much more space of my own here.

To help you decide, here are some pros and cons of living on hall:

Pros of living on hall:
- Close proximity to university/law school
- Relatively safe (24/7 guards)
- Affordable rent based on the type of room
- Opportunity to meet persons from different countries
- Free shuttle service to school (when the drivers aren't on strike or attitudinal)

Cons of living on hall:
- Small rooms
- Forced to share a room in certain halls
- Shared kitchen (people steal your food from the fridge, kitchens are often left dirty, someone is always cooking and hogging the best stove)
- Shared bathrooms (I think this speaks for itself - if not, here we go: few toilets and plenty asses, many people do not flush, the majority of the toilets do not work so you have to rush early for the working ones, when water goes it is a nightmare, the immature and/or confused male residents may pop in to the female bathrooms every now and then to irritate/scare the shit out of you - no pun intended)
- Shared common rooms (you can never find the TV remote, the TV often does not work, the couches smell, the rooms tend to be full of loud people, the AC is usually set to 'Antarctic')
- Very noisy and immature residents
- Constant parties and events (if you are a sociable person you may be fine with these)

Apartments:
This is probably the best option for law students. They are most definitely less noisy than living on a hall and much more private. The main cons may be the proximity to law school depending on the location of the apartment and higher rent (depending on the area, size and type of apartment). Safety may also be an issue, again depending on the location and whether or not it is in a gated community with a security system.

Living at Home:
If you are fortunate to live in the country where your law school is located, living at home has the great advantage of reducing your financial burdens. If you live with your parents, you would

most likely not be required to pay rent. At least you would not have the additional expense of paying rent to live on a hall of residence or in an apartment. And of course, home cooked food! The cons are likely to be that you may have greater family commitments, more distractions at home, and less sense of independence and privacy.

Now, these are not all the issues associated with the various types of available accommodation but hopefully they may assist you in making an informed decision, should you require a place to stay.

Supplies

You should also consider whether or not you will be buying books. Law books in general are very expensive. If you decide to buy your books, you should factor their cost in to your budget from the start. On average, one text book may cost between US $70.00 - US $100.00. A few may be less. Second hand books are usually cheaper, however, I always bought my books new. I always prefer brand new books with no markings or dog ears from previous readers.

Whether you can afford to buy your books may be your main consideration. Please be guided that you do not need to buy every single book on your book list. I did not buy every one but I tended to buy two per course, which in hindsight was quite an unnecessary expense, particularly when tutors denounced certain books after I had already bought them.

If you have no problem sharing books or using books that others have used, there is always the library. I bought my books to avoid having to fight for library books and having to return them when they were due, even though I had not finished using them. Just be warned that the good books are always in short supply and there is usually only one copy of the most sought after texts in the library - yes, one copy. Said copy also tends to take a long walk in the park, gets lost among the bushes and can never be found (a.k.a some selfish wretch beats you to it, takes it and never returns it, and/or removes it from its shelf and hides it among dusty old books that no one uses to prevent anyone else from finding it. Yes, these people exist in abundance in law school. More on these types later.)

Food

Assuming that you have completed university, you would know by now how vital a good diet is for studying. A good diet - healthy food. But on the average student's budget, this can be difficult to maintain, particularly as fast food is often quicker and cheaper to obtain. However, if you want to be at your optimum for studying, I would advise that you put fruits, vegetables, and vitamins into your budget.

Dress

Now, I do not know if your law school has a dress code but the one I attended certainly did. Whether or not you comply with the dress code is totally up to you. But be warned that non-compliance often leads to sidelong looks, snickers, and the development of an unsavoury reputation among your peers and tutors. In extreme cases, you can be reprimanded and suspended.

If you are required to wear suits, please wear suits. If your skirts must be a certain length, your pants a certain fit, please do not set foot on the premises dressed like a hooker or pimp (no offence to hookers and pimps). If you are required to wear only sober colours, please do so. You may have a very colourful personality and an exotic fashion sense, but law school is not the runway. Please save your costumes for the parties. You may rebel a bit, but do so in moderation and with good sense (I wore a pink checkered shirt and a peach shirt a couple times, but I knew not to wear them in certain classes).

Travel and Safety

In this day and age, wherever you go, your safety will always be an important consideration. I attended law school in a country notorious for its rising crime rate. But this did not prevent me from going out when I wanted to (piles of schoolwork did that). I was not much of a party-person but when I went out, I usually was not alone after dark. I was also fortunate to have my own transportation, which reduced the risks associated with public transportation.

However, if you have to use the bus/taxi you can still be safe. Just ensure that you tell a friend where you are going, use reputable, licensed taxis, be aware of your surroundings and stay away from neighbourhoods known for being crime zones. Do not travel with lots of money, keep your bus/taxi fare close at hand, do not count large sums of money in public, always be aware of your wallet/purse, and try and sit behind the taxi driver if you are ever alone in a taxi. You may also record the driver's license plate number and forward it to a friend as an extra precaution.

Relationships

As I mentioned previously, law school is very time-consuming. It will place a serious damper on your social life if you had one before. It may also put a strain on your relationships with friends, family and significant others as you would have less time to spend with them. However, it is possible to balance spending time with loved ones and your schoolwork, as many people have done it. As long as your people are aware of how demanding your studies are/will be and you do not neglect them completely, your relationships that are worth keeping should survive.

Chapter 3: The First Day, Week and Month

The First Day

It is your first day of law school. Are you excited, nervous, anxious? Most people usually are. The first time doing something new is always a bit daunting. The first day of law school is no different. It is the start of a new and life-altering chapter of your life.

If you willingly signed up for it, then you would probably feel some sort of excitement even if it is only a tiny glimmer. For the optimists, it is the start of new possibilities - the first day of your journey to accomplishing your goals. Now, you can imagine what the pessimists would think but let's not focus on them.

Welcome to law school!

What to Expect

The first day usually consists of a few orientation sessions. This is when you will meet the majority, if not all of your tutors and course directors. The principal and senior tutor would also make an appearance sometime during the day. During the introductory sessions, the course directors will try very hard to employ varying scare tactics on you. They will attempt to intimidate you and make you second guess your decision to enrol (if you did not have doubts before). Do not let them burst your bubble or defeat you. There may be a couple 'nice' ones but many of them live off of your fear and anxiety. Do not feed them.

You may also be assigned your class groupings on this day and a provisional timetable for your classes. You may be disheartened to see that you were not placed in the same group as the majority of your friends (if you had friends from university who enrolled in the same law school). But do not let this be an obstacle to your performance. You can and will survive without them. In fact, you will be better off as they will not pose a distraction to you during your classes. Having friends in different class groups can also be beneficial to you later on (you can get their notes and compare them with your own to see if the content differ). You will also have the opportunity to meet new people and gain new acquaintances.

On the topic of friends and new acquaintances, you will also see the peacocks out and about in their glory. These are the showoffs who you may know from your undergraduate years, or the new ones who may irritate your bones, if you let them. You know the type. The ones decked head to toe in designer suits, heels and runway makeup, talking the loudest, grinning the broadest and just generally making a flamboyant effort to be seen. They will claim that they are so excited and that they know the course directors personally. They crave attention. Do not give them the time of day.

By the end of the day, if all goes well you may still feel hopeful. Congratulations! You have survived the first day. Go home and prepare yourself for the coming week.

The First Week

The first week of law school is similar to the first day, in my experience. In my day, it mainly consisted of orientation sessions and a few of the classes were actually cancelled for various administrative reasons. But perhaps things have improved since then. If not, you are likely to have a few introductory classes and meet the majority of your classmates. The pace may be slow as ever and you may wonder if you really are attending law school.

Please be aware that this first week will be the slowest and only week like it. Take advantage of the slow pace and free class periods by reading ahead and organising your files. Time will start to fly and the pace will increase before you know it. Prepare yourself mentally.

The First Month

Your classes should be in full swing by the ending of the first month. Consequently, your work load should be much heavier now as well. You would have met all of your group mates and would be familiar with your class dynamics. You ought to know by now who are the class clowns, the nerds, the suck-ups and the ones who just blend into the background. You would also be more familiar with your tutors and their various idiosyncrasies.

The showoffs and the fakers will be out and about, claiming that their tutors have given them so much work to do and that they do not know how they will get it all done. They will be asking you about your study schedule and what works best for you, while giving you vague and sketchy details about theirs.

They are leeches and backstabbers. Their main aim is to try to dishearten and demotivate you so that your productivity will suffer, giving them a better chance of achieving the highest grades to make it on to the honour roll at the end of the year. Yes, there are people like this and the majority of them are in law school. Try to avoid them.

What Next

During this first month, you should try your best to read ahead of each class's topics as much as possible. Now, 'read ahead' does not mean that you have to read every single book or material on each topic. You will never finish or go nuts if you try. Just read from the main sources and pick a few reference books to supplement your reading. Make notes along the way if you normally do so.

If you have not done so already, now would be the best time to gather as much material as you can for each course from your friends or colleagues. A couple weeks before I began law school, a very generous friend of mine emailed me a vast file of documents that was complied over the years by past law students. It contained cases, case notes, briefs, lecture notes, audio recordings, samples of old assignments, and many other invaluable documents. It was very useful and I often turned to it as one of my first points of reference. Upon request, I also received similar documents from a friend who had graduated two years before me. Make sure to get your hands on similar notes. They will save you a lot of time and stress trying to find the information all on your own.

While you gather your material and organise yourself, you should also discuss topics and ideas with your friends/colleagues. Find out from persons in other class groups how far their tutors have reached in the syllabus and compare notes if you can. Now would also be the best time to start to develop a good relationship with the nerds. They will be easy to spot; they usually live in the library or empty classrooms.

On that note, make sure to familiarise yourself with your school's library as well. As I had bought the majority of my course books, I had no real need to utilise the library except when it was assignment time and I needed to borrow the odd book or do some extra research. But please do not underestimate the usefulness of the library. Nor the library staff. Introduce yourself to them and be polite and humble; humility goes a long way.

You should also go to the main office and make it a priority to meet the principal and the senior tutor. Why? Because you need to be seen and known to exist, and you need to have powerful people on your side. How do you think all the suck-ups and fakers excel and get the best jobs after graduation? Connections!

Now, I am not saying to be like the suck-ups and fakers. You do not have to become bosom buddies with the principal or senior tutor. No. Just establish a good relationship - one in which they know your name so they would be more likely to assist you should you need their help later on.

Similarly, take this time to meet the office administrative staff and be polite and friendly. They can be very useful around assignment and exam time when you may need a favour.

Chapter 4: Assignments

If the first week appeared to crawl by, the first month will be over before you know it. And then guess what is next? The start of probably the most torturous aspect of law school. Assignment time. Assignments, assignments, assignments... There will seem to be no end.

Assignments will be issued faster than you know it. In my time, a couple years ago, assignments were issued every two weeks. You may think that is a lot of time in which to do your assignments but in reality, it is not. Believe me, I know from experience.

When you get the first assignment you read it, you may not even take it seriously and decide, "I'll just check it tomorrow or the next day." But the thing is, you have four, five, maybe six courses and the work begins to pile up so fast that you forget about the assignments sometimes until it is too late. Procrastination is the enemy of success. Do not let this happen to you.

In order to handle assignments successfully, there are several things that you need to do. Here is how to handle them:

How to Handle Assignments

Mental Preparation

First of all, you need to be mentally prepared. This means that you should have a serious conversation with yourself. Adopt the mindset that assignment time is very important. Assignments count towards your final grade. They determine overall whether or not you will pass your courses and thus be able to graduate from law school. You need to take assignments seriously. They are not optional. You must do them otherwise you will fail. So be prepared.

Although some assignments may seem very short in terms of what they are asking you to do, there is always a trick or some underlying issue that is not clear on the face and you need to read more into it. Take every line of every question seriously. Do not underestimate any course just because many people tell you that it is easy, and that you do not have to spend much time on it. No. Regard every assignment and every course as equally important as the others.

Around assignment time you will also find the fakers coming out in their numbers. They will also be claiming that, "Oh, the assignment is so hard!" or that they do not understand what to do in an effort to try and overwhelm you and make you feel frustrated. This is especially unnerving when you think that you have figured something out and then they tell you that they don't know what they're doing and that it seems so hard. It is a tactic to try to make you doubt yourself. Do not let them get to you. Ignore them as much as possible. People who only whine and complain and who do not offer to assist you, are not people with whom you should associate. They only do what they do for their own selfish reasons. So, again, avoid the fakers during assignment time. In fact, avoid them totally if you can. You can hear what they say, just do not listen.

Start Early

Now, what to do? You need to start early. This is crucial. Start working on your assignments as soon as you get them. I was guilty of not doing that. I may have started a few days later and in the end it built more pressure on me. Unless you are a person who prefers to work under pressure and you excel under pressure, by all means, work late. But if you really want to do well, if you want to succeed and pass your assignments and get good enough grades, you need to pace yourself and put the required amount of work and effort into your assignments. In order to do so, you need to work on the assignments as early as possible.

'Early' means the very same day that you get the assignment. You may be busy but hey, remind yourself that it has to be done. What you should do is set a reminder on your phone or on your laptop - whatever device that you normally have at hand; in today's age it would be your cellphones. Select whatever application that you use for alerts. Set a reminder that you have to start your assignment today. And actually do it when your alarm goes off. This does not mean that you have to write out and do all the research and everything on the same day. No. At least read through the question and try to understand what it requires. You can begin to make your notes as to how to proceed at this stage.

Focus

You also need to focus. The period before assignments would have been more introductory as to what law school is and what to expect. But now you need to completely do away with distractions. At least while you are trying to get the meat of your assignments out of the way. This is similar for all aspects of studying. When you know that you have serious work to do, shut off the TV, and put away whatever electronic games you play. Turn off your cellphone or put it on silent. Stop gossiping with other people. Stop going out and liming and partying so much. Focus on your task, which is completing your assignments and doing well. Afterwards, you can take a break and resume all your pleasurable activities.

Collaborate

Another important thing to do during assignment time is to collaborate. You may not be a very people-friendly person, or you may prefer to study and work on your own. That may have worked well for you in your undergraduate years but at law school it is a different ballgame. I was one such person who preferred to work on my own which I did throughout my undergraduate years at university. I also did that mostly for law school, but at law school I realized that working on your own, being a lone ranger, will not get you the results that you want. Very few people succeed working isolated - completely isolated, that is. Especially with assignments, you need to work with others. You need to bounce ideas off of colleagues and friends. See how they interpret the question. They may have a completely different interpretation from yours. They may raise issues that you never thought of. They may give you cases and articles that you did not find or were not able to find. So it is very useful to talk to other people about the assignments to see how they plan to approach it. To see what they can do to help you and in turn what you can do to help them.

Of course, be wise regarding who you work with. At this point you should be able to pick out the fakers, those who just want to try and bring you down. The leeches as well - you should know who they are by now. Stay away from those who just want to suck all your energy and information from you and give nothing back to you in return. Find a group of people you can trust relatively well enough. Those who you know from reputation to have a good head on their shoulders; those who are sensible enough not to give you the wrong information and are hard-working, and willing to put in the effort and not just hide whatever research they find and keep it to themselves. Yes, there are those people. Especially in law school.

So collaboration is key. You want to succeed and have a well-rounded answer for your questions. Remember with law school, everything is analysis. Argue both sides in most situations. Of course, there are those instances where there must be only one answer and that is where collaboration is very useful as well. The views of friends or other classmates may help to guide you in the right direction.

Thus, working with others is very important. Yes, you may not be a very sociable person but this is the time when you have to push away your insecurities, your fears of talking in groups, your fears wondering what people think about you. That does not matter at this point in time. All you should be concerned with is how to pass your exams, your assignments, how to do well and get out of law school with your qualifications. So if you have to fake being friendly, fake being sociable, fake the qualities of an outgoing, people-friendly person then do it, because this is for your benefit in the long run. I'm not saying to become a faker. No. Work on the positive attributes. Just adopt the skills necessary in order to do what you have to do to succeed and get the grades that you need to pass and survive law school.

Avoid Plagiarism

Now, you also need to be aware of avoiding plagiarism. You should know what that is by now - taking other people's work wholesale and submitting it as your own. Even if you do not have the intention of plagiarism it could still be regarded as such if you do not give the original authors of the work their due recognition. You can avoid plagiarism by simply explaining definitions and issues in your own words. Your analysis would be dependent on how you analyze the facts, the issues, the law and your application of these to the problem questions.

There is also the issue of plagiarising other students' work. Do not do that. I remember in my day, there were two students who were either suspended or expelled from law school for being found guilty of plagiarism. They allegedly both submitted the same assignment answer. They got kicked out of law school. You do not want that to be you.

So even if you work together with a friend or colleague make sure that what you submit is your work. Do not allow your friend or whoever else to copy your work directly. You may have the same issues, the same way of applying and analyzing, but put it in your own words please. At this point, you need to be building and protecting your reputation. You do not want to start off your law career being known as a thief or a plagiarist - even before you graduate from law school. There are too may bad lawyers out there. Do not become one of them. Do not cultivate such immoral conduct. At least not so early in the game. Well, actually, not at all.

Handling Conflict: Group Assignments

There will most likely come a time when you will be compelled to do group assignments. Very few people I know enjoyed these; I was not one of them. In my experience, the most challenging aspect of group assignments was dealing with the various conflicting personalities of some of the group members. You would likely know by now that there are different types of students. There are the hard-workers and those who hardly work; these can be subdivided into many categories.

I was the leader of my assignment group in first year, and only three of us, out of six, did the majority of the work. When it came time to evaluate each member's performance, and I gave an honest evaluation, one of the slackers had the audacity to argue with me about her mark; she had contributed the least. I maintained my composure for the sake of peace.

Similarly for you, do not lose your cool in the likely event that you find yourself forced to work with a group of slackers and leeches. I know it can be very frustrating, especially as their performance or lack thereof will affect your overall assignment grade. Do not let anyone goad you into verbal or physical altercations. Walk away or ignore them if necessary. If you cannot resolve the conflict yourself, direct your issues to your group leader or your tutor. Your last resort would be the senior tutor or the principal. Hopefully, you will not have to resort to them.

The powers at be (the administration) claim that the purpose of group work is to prepare you to be able to work with difficult attorneys after law school. It may be true in some instances.

How to Deal with Failure

In my day, the assignment grades were posted up on the notice board. You had to match your ID number with your grade. They would all be listed chronologically. It used to be such pain and torture waiting for the assignment results to come out; I used to be filled with dread and anticipation, hoping and pleading that I passed. And not just passed, hoping that I got an A. So of course, on the occasions when I actually saw that I got an A, I would be filled with excitement and joy.

Now, on the reverse side is when you get a grade that you did not expect. Bad grades. In my day, an A, B, and C were the passes. D was a fail. Now, how do you deal with the bad grades? Perhaps by now you may be used to getting different kinds of grades so you may have experience with failure. But for those of you who do not, this tip is for you.

I did not have experience with any major failure in school until year one at law school. To be precise, it was the first assignment for the Criminal Practice and Procedure course, which the majority of persons in my year claimed was so easy. It was a popular view that the Criminal Law course was so easy to pass, and that hardly anybody failed. So when I got back my grade and I saw that the vast majority of the students were awarded A's and B's and I counted and saw that maybe less than 10 people had failed and I was among the 10, my heart stopped and my body went cold. Needless to say, I was horrified.

I had always been a straight A student, all the way from primary school to secondary school. I topped my classes at sixth form. I did well enough in university having graduated with upper second class honours. I was actually rather close to getting first class honours, which I could have gotten if I had put more work into it and had learned the secrets to getting A's earlier. So I am just giving you a background to highlight the fact that I was not used to failure.

Thus, it was a big shock, a big slap in the face. It felt like a gut-wrenching pain that day when I got back my results for this very first assignment for Criminal Practice and Procedure. It was a problem type question, as most of them were and apparently I had misinterpreted what was required; I had the wrong issues and was marked down for that. I requested a review for my paper and it still came back with the failing grade. To this day, I still remember the day that assignment grade came out; I had to do a Trial Advocacy presentation. I was so depressed. I did not know how to get through it but somehow I managed. That day was probably the worst day of my experience in law school. At least, up to that point.

Of course I cried. It hurt. It pained like a physical wound but it was an emotional wound. I am telling you all this to say that it was my first failure in school and it felt terrible. But I did not just suck sorrow and bawl constantly. I just cried that one day. Fortunately for me, I had the support of my parents and family. I spoke to my mother, got advice about it and realised that it was not the end of the world. In fact, what that failure did was motivate me to work even harder on the Criminal Practice and Procedure Law course itself because I never liked that course. I only liked criminal law at university. But when it came to law school, I did not like it. I did not understand why people thought it was so easy. Perhaps I just did not have a mind for it. I don't know. But that very first failure actually put me off the course for a while. But at the same time it motivated me to work harder to make sure I never failed another assignment again.

And in fact, I never failed another assignment in law school. That failure actually forced me to realize how important it is to work and collaborate with others because up to that point I had been working on all my assignments on my own, not bouncing ideas off of others. Not in group chats for assignments. Nothing like that. So after that failing grade, I made sure I collaborated with as many people as possible.

In fact, my class (Group 8) was a very supportive and friendly bunch. I remember one time after class, we were all discussing the assignment and how to answer it. One very helpful classmate gave us the main case, which was directly related to the issue and the question. I went home, researched it and it was in fact the correct case so he was not feeding us bullshit. It was accurate and in fact his help and the help of others assisted me in getting an A in the next assignment. In fact I got another

A in the final assignment as well (each course had three assignments). So although I failed the first assignment in Criminal Practice and Procedure, I got As in the next two assignments. This raised my overall grade to a B.

So hey, although you may have started off with a failure, that does not mean that you will end in failure. As long as you have the right attitude. Don't beat yourself up. Don't suck sorrow. Take the failure as a learning experience. Do what you have to do in order to improve and stay motivated. You are not a failure. You are not defined by your grades. A failing grade simply means that you perhaps interpreted something wrong. It was a mistake and you will learn from your mistakes. Move on, improve and be better.

Failing is not the end of the world. In fact, it makes you stronger. In my case it made me re-think my studying tactics and work habits, because I was not a person who liked crowds or liked to study with other people. It made me realize that sometimes you have to do what you do not like to do if it is the method that will work in your best interest. So use the methods that work. Do not be stubborn, pig-headed and think that your way is the only way. Do what you need to do in order to succeed. Improve yourself and of course, help others along the way.

Chapter 5: Tutors

A quick note about Tutors. They are there to guide your analysis, to engage with you, to foster and facilitate discussions on the subject material that you are responsible for reading and analyzing. The tutors are not there to teach you as a normal teacher in Primary School or High School would. This is not the spoon-feeding stage as you should realize by now. Their main purpose is to clarify any questions you may have about the course that you are pursuing.

What to Expect

Now, what should you expect from your tutors? As I said before, do not expect them to spoon-feed you. You are responsible for the majority of your learning at this point. You have to do lots and lots of reading on your own as you will know from your undergraduate years. It is simply a good deal more this time around at law school.

The Helpful Tutors

However, some tutors can be very helpful. I would advise you to make as much use as possible of these helpful tutors. Ask them questions, get your answers; do not be afraid to speak up. If you do not want to ask them questions in class, email them. Some of them even give you their phone numbers. Of course, do not abuse the privilege. Put your tutors to good use - that is what they are there for. Their purpose is to help you. They are being paid to answer your questions and guide your analysis and your understanding of the subject material.

Some of the tutors have office hours and you can make an appointment to see them privately to discuss any issues that you may have with the course. Many of them are helpful in that regard and would make time to actually go through questions that you have, and guide you. Most of them also accept questions that you have written out; they would read your answers and correct it, and give you guidance as to how to improve.

I would highly advise that you take these opportunities to practice answering past exam paper questions and submit your answers to your tutors. Our education system basically prepares students to answer exam questions and it is the same with law school. It is not all that practical, really. It is about passing your exams. And practicing past exam paper questions is the key to succeeding in your exams so that you know what to expect.

As the persons who mark your exam papers are the tutors, it is wise to submit your answers to them for marking and guidance. It is good practice in preparation for your exams and it will help you to see exactly what you understand. You may think that you understand a concept, but when it comes to actually explaining it in writing, it might be a bit difficult if you lack sufficient experience in answering questions according to whatever guidelines the particular course requires.

So practicing exams past papers and submitting your answers to your tutors is very wise. Again, I strongly advise that you do so. I only did this a few times and if I had to do law school all over again, I would make sure that I wrote many more questions to submit to my tutors in all the courses. I am sure that I would have done much better if I practiced more past exam papers and gotten more feedback from tutors. This is VERY important. I cannot emphasize this enough.

The Unfriendly Tutors

Now, on the other hand, there are the cranky and unfriendly tutors. They are not all like this but a good deal of them are. And you know how life is when you have a whole lot of positives and then one or a few negatives. The negatives tend to overshadow the positives. But do not let that happen to you. Tutors are humans and they have their bad days just like everyone else. Some of their crankiness and hostility may be due to temporary issues. Who knows? Maybe they are having problems at home, car troubles, health issues or financial problems. Maybe they are wondering whether teaching is the right career for them. You never know.

But then again, you have the tutors who seem to be permanently cold and aloof. Or the course directors who are naturally hostile. Their hostility is not a temporary issue. It is who they are and ingrained in their bones. One stands out in my mind clearly. She was the type of course director who seemed to revel in the fact that her course had the highest failure rate. Tutors like her seemed to want to make you fail. They seemed to find joy in the fact that you may not understand what you are doing. But do not let them deter you or make you feel badly about yourself.

On the path to greatness there are many stumbling blocks. These hostile tutors probably have some serious psychological or emotional issues. They may have experienced some trauma when they were younger. They may have had tutors who were even worse than they were. Their harsh treatment of you may be some way of theirs to soothe their own damaged and frail psyche. Do not hate them, but pity them. Try to avoid any conflict with such tutors.

If they are strict about a certain way in which you should answer questions, please follow their guidelines. Remember your purpose of being in law school, which is to fulfill the requirements of your course, pass your exams, get your Legal Education Certificate and get the hell out. You are not there to argue with rigid and obstinate tutors. Be humble and in this instance follow the path of least resistance. Always think of the long-term consequences.

In the unfortunate event that you happen to have conflict with one of these tutors, try and resolve it as best and as humbly as you can. Be mature. Be the one to apologize and try to move on. You want to avoid any distractions, any unpleasantness that would negatively affect your performance in your assignments and ultimately, your exams. You know, some tutors can hold a grudge. Do not make things worse by prolonging the conflict.

You are only a student at this stage. I am sure that you are probably not the child of a Prime Minister or some powerful government official. In other words, your tutor is king right now and you are the serf. Bow and scrape until you can knock that king off his throne and take it over.

If you happen to be involved in any conflict with your tutors, at least it would be a learning experience and it should open your eyes to the fact that your tutors are not unique; they are probably all lawyers and they are examples of the types of lawyers that we have in society today. But do not lose hope. There are still some good ones out there.

Chapter 6: Networking

It is very important that you start networking at an early stage. As in, right now. Why? Well, if you plan on practicing law after you graduate, and especially if you plan to go into private practice and basically set up shop on your own, networking is key to your survival. It is key to getting clients, to making links with other attorneys and other influential people who may in turn, give you some guidance, maybe even pass on useful precedents to you and even pass on clients.

The more people you know, and the more people who you share a good working relationship with, the greater your chances are of building your client base and establishing yourself in the legal profession. And of course, networking is very crucial if you want to get a good job. But then again, you can try and link up with as many people as possible but that does not guarantee that you will get a job after graduation. But let's not despair at this point. Let us focus on the immediate future, which is surviving year one of law school.

Ways to Network

Now, how should you network? One way you can do so is by joining study groups. This should work for those who study well in groups. If you do not have a group of friends who you knew from your undergraduate years, well this is time to create a new group. Start talking with the persons in your class. Especially find the "nerds", as I advised earlier. Link up with them fast. Start establishing a relationship of trust and confidence and you may later on find out who their friends are. They may introduce you to other people and you will build your links.

Apart from the nerds, have good relationships with your tutors. Your tutors are lawyers and at some point, they would have worked in the legal profession. So they should have links to be able to connect you with other attorneys as well. And many of your tutors are judges who would have vast connections. Get on their good side. But do not be an irritating, kiss-ass bum fly. You know the type that I mean.

You should also get to know some of the staff members, those in key positions as well as those who work behind the counter, the clerks and the library staff. Strike up a conversation with some of them. Find out what their interests are, their hobbies. Relate to them on a personable, human level. They can be very useful contacts after you graduate.

You can also join extracurricular groups such as the environmental club, debate groups, and the human rights group, of which I was a member. Entering competitions is also a good way to network as well. Even if you do not get very far in them, it would at least give you an opportunity to talk to other students and those who moderate the competitions. Maybe you may have moved on to the next level which would give you the chance to meet with students from other law schools. That would be a great opportunity to make connections with students and professionals from other jurisdictions in the Caribbean, and maybe even around the world.

Attending legal events is also a great way to network. Look out for any events or seminars that are held by your law school or by the University of the West Indies or any other local institution on legal matters. If time permits, attend a few of these. Ask questions, go and talk to the hosts of the events. Introduce yourself and start building your links.

To be successful at networking you need to be sociable. You need to be friendly, or at least try to interact with others. This may be difficult for some people. I know it was difficult for me because I am naturally reserved and not all that sociable. But in this profession you are forced to do things that require a lot of human interaction. If you are strongly against it, well you may just be in the wrong profession. If you are reserved and prefer quiet company, networking will test your comfort zone. However, at the same time it is useful for helping you to increase your confidence, your people skills and your communication skills. Just take it one step at a time. Start now.

Chapter 7: Student Issues

We all know that law school is a lot of work and can be very stressful. There may come a time where you may be facing some difficult situations which may make surviving law school very challenging. To name a few, some of those issues may include:

- Financial problems;
- Health issues;
- Issues related to stress;
- Family or personal problems;
- Emotional issues such as depression; and
- Problems related to conflicts with friends and other relationships.

There may be many other problems that students face but these are the most common.

How to Manage Your Issues

Financial Problems:

Regarding financial problems, you should set a budget for yourself if you have not done so already. If you have set a budget, try and return to it. See if you could alter the budget if you have to or put yourself on a strict regimen to follow it. If you are in dire financial straits, you can take a small loan from a lending institution like a bank or a credit union. Many of those institutions offer small loans which are relatively easy to obtain for students.

You can also seek help from your friends (assuming that you have friends) and family members as well. Do not allow your pride to get the best of you or hamper your studies. Put your pride away and let others know that you are facing financial difficulties. Ask for a little help out. Ask for a loan. Specify that it is not a gift and let them know that you fully intend to repay them. This may be a good time to practice your legal drafting skills. Draft up a contract for repayment.

In the event that you cannot obtain a loan from your friends or a financial institution, you can also consider approaching your church. In addition, there are student groups that are formed for the purpose of helping students who are in financial difficulties. Again, do not let your pride get the best of you. It may be awkward or uncomfortable for you to ask for help, but when you need help you need to ask for it. People cannot read your mind to know that you are unable to afford to perhaps buy your next meal or pay your rent. So ask for help in order to get help.

I was fortunate to have had the financial support of my parents throughout my education and even up to law school. Some of you may also be that fortunate, but for those of you who are not, obtaining the necessary finances may be a bit difficult. Please consider all the avenues available to you to obtain financial assistance before making the drastic decision to withdraw from law school. There may even be options available to you to apply for scholarships. Keep your eyes and ears open to seek out every available opportunity that would benefit you.

Health Issues:

If you have a serious medical condition which is likely to negatively impact your studying, you should perhaps get the advice of a doctor as to whether or not you should be pursuing the difficult task of attempting to obtain your legal education certificate. If the condition is related to your heart, you should think twice before putting yourself under the constraints of having to study law at this time.

If it is not such a serious condition and it can be managed through lifestyle habits, consider changing your diet. Whether or not you have a medical condition, it is always best to maintain good health especially when you are studying. The average student's lifestyle is mainly sedentary. When closed up indoors all day studying, many students do not get much fresh air; and then their diets tend to be poor because of time constraints and mismanaged budgets. Thus, it is vital that you consider monitoring your diet; eat healthy.

Additionally, you should eat at the right times. Several research studies suggest that eating meals late at night can negatively affect your body. For example, when you eat at late hours your metabolism slows down and you may not digest food as quickly or as efficiently as during the daylight hours. Some studies even suggest that eating late at night can increase your risk of gaining weight and developing obesity (Baron et al., 2011; Penn Medicine News, 2017).

Incidentally, do not starve yourself. Just make sure that you are eating at least three times a day. Eat vegetables, fruits, and take multivitamins. It is very important that you take vitamins but do not overdo your self-medication.

Stress-related Issues:

For stress-related problems, I would advise that you seek counselling early, especially if it is a matter which is troubling you emotionally. Your law school should have a counsellor available. The counsellor is there to assist you with your emotional issues and any other issues affecting your student life. Do not be afraid to seek the help that you need. Make an appointment. It is usually free. The purpose of counsellors is to help you and whatever you tell them is confidential. There is no stigma attached to seeking help. At this stage, you need to protect not only your physical health, but your mental health as well. You need to take the necessary steps to reduce your stress.

If you prefer not to seek a professional counsellor, talk to someone else instead. Find someone you can trust, whether it is a family member or a close friend. Perhaps even a tutor. Speak to them about your issues - whatever it is that you are dealing with that is causing you pain or that is distracting you, hampering your progress with your studies. Talk to someone about it. They can offer you advice and help you overcome such difficulties. You need to let people know that you are in distress. Let them know so that they can assist you.

Ways to Reduce Your Stress:

Here are some steps to help you reduce your stress.

- **Exercise.** The student life tends to be a sedentary one and it is very important to get exercise to keep yourself healthy, keep your blood flowing. It allows you to breathe some fresh air if you are exercising outside. Getting up and moving gives you a break from studying and your stressful environment. Exercising is a major way to reduce your stress which has been proven many and many times.

- **Change your diet.** As I advised earlier, eating healthy foods will help you. If you eat less sugary and fatty foods, you will feel better and you will gain more energy to study.

- **Meditation and prayer.** These are also effective ways of reducing stress. When you wake up, you can sit quietly and reflect on your thoughts - what you want to do for the day, what you want to achieve. Think positively. Repeat a few mantras and centre yourself. Similarly, you could also try prayer if you are a spiritual person. Pray for the strength to survive law school. Pray for the strength to overcome difficulties and your challenges. Pray for strength. Pray for wisdom. Pray for guidance.

- **Practice controlled breathing.** You can do various breathing exercises which would help to steady your heart-rate. This helps especially if you are an anxious person, if you are nervous, or if you get high-strung or upset very easily. It is similar to meditation where you keep calm and quiet and concentrate on your breathing. Concentrate on being calm and still. This will help you to reduce your stress.

- **Do something fun.** Take time for your favourite hobby, whether you like to draw, dance, sing, write music, watch movies, play sports, do martial arts, go fishing, swim, do craft work, play an instrument. Whatever it is that you like to do, take some time and do it. Have fun. Ease the stress. But of course, everything in moderation.

- **Laugh.** Laughing is probably one of the best medicines. Similarly to doing something fun, find a show or joke or something that will make you feel better. Something that will just make you burst out laughing. Laughing is really a good way to relieve your stress, even if it is only temporary.

- **Talk to your friends and family.** Find some time to spend with your loved ones. This may be part of doing something fun. But devote some time to your friends, your family, people who care about you. Do not stay isolated in a bubble just studying, studying, studying. Go and hang out with your family, your friends. Go on a date. Have fun. Enjoy yourself. But again, in moderation.

- **Do not over-think things/ do not overwhelm yourself.** If you tend to be a worrier (like I am, unfortunately, but I am working on it) you may become stressed very easily. It is important that you control your thoughts; you control how far you think about things. Do not over-stress. Make a list of the things that you can handle - the things that you can deal with right now in your circumstance. And do not think too far into the future. There is only so much that you can control. Take things one step at a time.

- **Medicine.** This should be a last resort when all else fails and you definitely need something to reduce your stress. There is always medicine but I would advise that you have it prescribed by a doctor.

Block out the issues:

Another way in which you can deal with your many problems is by blocking them out. If you feel that your problems are too overwhelming, if you feel as if they will completely take over your life and they will completely distract you from your studying, try and block them out, if possible. If you cannot block them out and they become very serious, perhaps you should consider taking some time off from school if that is a possibility. Worse-case scenario, you may just have to withdraw from school and defer to another academic year. However, hopefully, your situation will not be as dire.

A Little Pep Talk:

In conclusion, despite the fact that you may be facing several issues, perhaps of varying severity, if you put your mind to it and you persevere, and you continue to be dedicated and focused, you can survive law school despite your many challenges. Just remember that no matter what you are facing, there is always someone who faced the same problems and probably under even harsher conditions than what you are facing right now. That by no means belittles whatever situation you are in; it just gives perspective to the fact that, yes your dilemma may seem to be terribly difficult, but it is not impossible to overcome.

You may feel stressed beyond all limits but you are not alone. Most people who went through law school had to deal with many issues, perhaps of varying severity but we all had issues to deal with and yours is not unique, whatever it may be. There is always a solution to the problem.

When you feel like quitting just remind yourself why you started studying law in the first place. What was your motivation? Let the answer be your guide. Let it be the motivator to give you the little encouragement that you need in order to continue along your journey and survive law school. It is only two years. You can do it.

Yes, the journey is hard. It is difficult. It is a lot of tears, a lot of sweat, perhaps a little bit of blood. But getting your legal education certificate, getting your qualification in the end will be worth it. No matter what, that cannot be taken away from you even if you do not actually pursue a law career in the end. What you are facing right now will prepare you for the future. Facing difficulties and enduring them, overcoming them, makes you a stronger person.

You are only in law school for a time - two years at the minimum. Before you know it, it will be over. Like my grandmother always told me, "This too shall pass." Yes, it may be difficult. Yes, it is difficult. But to quote my late uncle, who quoted my mother, "Gold is purified through fire." Your strength of character is conceived and developed through adversity.

You can do it. And you will!

Useful References:

For advice on eating:
Baron, K. G., Reid, K. J., Kern, A. S., & Zee, P. C. (2011). Role of Sleep Timing in Caloric Intake and BMI. Obesity: A Research Journal, 19(7), 1374-1381. **https://onlinelibrary.wiley.com/doi/full/10.1038/oby. 2011.100**

Penn Medicine News. (2017). Timing Meals Later at Night Can Cause Weight Gain and Impair Fat Metabolism. Retrieved from **https://www.pennmedicine.org/news/news-releases/2017/june/timing-meals-later-at-night-can-cause-weight-gain-and-impair-fat-metabolism**

Advice on exercise and stress:
Melnick, M. (2013). How Does Exercise Reduce Stress? HuffPost. Retrieved from **https://www.huffingtonpost.com/2013/05/21/exercis**

e-reduces-stress-levels-anxiety-cortisol_n_3307325.html

Weir, K. (2011). The exercise effect. Monitor on Psychology, 42(11): 48. **http://www.apa.org/monitor/2011/12/exercise.aspx**

An easy to read resource on eating habits and mood:
Mind. (2015). Food and Mood. Retrieved from **https://www.mind.org.uk/information-support/tips-for-everyday-living/food-and-mood/#.WyPSEfZFw2w**

A YouTube video for guided meditation:
12 Minute Meditation to Reduce Stress Yoga with Fightmaster Yoga. [Video file]. Retrieved from **https://www.youtube.com/watch?v=mbx46jc9uaA**

Short article on the benefits of meditation:
Corliss, J. (2014). Mindfulness meditation may ease anxiety, mental stress. Retrieved from **https://www.health.harvard.edu/blog/mindfulness-meditation-may-ease-anxiety-mental-stress-201401086967**

Facebook page for the Mindful magazine:
https://www.facebook.com/mindfulorg/

Social support and stress:
American Psychological Association. (n.d.). Manage stress: Strengthen your support network. Retrieved from **http://www.apa.org/helpcenter/emotional-support.aspx**

A guide on how to start your day right:
See my blog at **https://www.gisellemills.com/**

Chapter 8: How to Study Effectively

(This topic originally appeared as an article on my blog at **gisellemills.com**)

Have you ever studied very hard but still did not receive the results that you wanted? It's frustrating after devoting so much time to your studies, isn't it? You may even have wondered if there was something wrong with you.

However, the real issue was probably not your intellectual ability but your study methods. There is a difference between studying and studying effectively. What you need to know is how to do the latter. This is particularly important for law school where proper time management is key.

Here are 12 tips on how to study effectively to help you get the grades you deserve.

1.   **Positive attitude:** This is a must. You need to have a positive attitude about your abilities and your success. Tell yourself that you are capable of passing your exams and doing well. You have to be your biggest cheerleader. Negative thoughts breed negative energy, which will ultimately negatively affect your exam performance. So think positively

about yourself and your capabilities. Your thoughts alone can direct your path to success.

2.   Avoid distractions: If you want to study effectively, you must avoid distractions as much as possible. You would know what are your biggest distractions; avoid them. Whether it's your friends, your cell phone, TV, electronics, going out, watching movies or shows, and/or gossiping – cut them out completely if you can. You would be surprised how much time you can save and dedicate towards effective studying instead.

3.   Study early in the term: You need to start your studying as early as possible. Do not procrastinate about this. This is often the downfall of many students. Do not be one of them. Do not rely on your perceived cramming skills. Start studying early so that you can pace yourself and avoid feeling overwhelmed when you leave all of your studying until the last minute.

4.   Study smart: If you want to study effectively, you have to study smart. This involves tailoring your study methods to suit each course and knowing how much material to cover. You need to know what each course entails and it would be useful to refer to your course outlines for this purpose.

In addition, many tutors/lecturers have their own particular quirks and requirements for doing well in their courses. If your tutors/lecturers are the ones who set your exams, and they are the fussy or nitpicky type, ensure that you study according to what each one of them wants. If Mr. A prefers his students to write in a particular style, do so. If Mrs. B hates fluff and prefers you to get straight to the point in your essays, do so. Do not give them any opportunity to deduct marks from you. As annoying as it may be, abide by their idiosyncrasies – it is only for a time.

5. **Use a study method that works best for you:** You should know yourself better than anyone. Thus, you should know by now which method of study works best for you. Are you a visual person who needs to draw things out to understand the concepts? Do you need to study with music or do you prefer silence? Do you study better in a group or by yourself? Does talking out loud help you remember better? Or do you study best by re-reading the material and writing? Stick to the method that works most effectively for you. Do not compromise this to please anyone else.

6. **Study at your optimum absorption time:** Are you an early bird or a night owl? Do you retain information better when you study during the day or at night? For me, I have always been an owl; for as long as I can remember I have always studied best and been most productive at night. Again, stick to what works best for you. Identify your most productive time of day and use it for your study sessions.

7. **Set time limits for studying:** Sometimes it is hard to stop when you are on a roll but it is important that you set time limits for studying. When you study for several hours at a time you will eventually begin to overwhelm yourself and become frustrated from trying to take in so much information in one long continuous stretch. Your mind will become oversaturated. To study effectively, you should study for no more than one or two hours at a time. Always be conscious of your mental health.

8. **Take breaks/get rest:** It is essential that you take breaks frequently when studying. Once you set your time limits for studying, stick to them and take a break when you have reached your study limit. Your mind needs time to recover. Also ensure that you get proper rest by sleeping for at least 6 – 8 hours per night. When it comes down to crunch time, I know that many students sacrifice sleep. Sometimes I would only get four hours and would be even more tired in the morning. Do not make this a habit. Your body needs good sleep to help you feel refreshed in the morning. You will be better able to retain more information when you are well-rested.

9.   Get help: If you are struggling to understand a concept or just need assistance with revision, get help from a tutor or classmate. This is not the time to be bashful or self-conscious; there is nothing wrong with asking for help. In fact, the students who score the best grades usually do so with the aid of extra tuition (some of course, also do so with the use of insider information). Many of these 'top' students keep this fact a secret, preferring to have you think that their performance was solely due to their intellectual abilities.

10.   Practise past exam papers: This is part of 'studying smart'. As mentioned in a previous chapter, the best way to prepare for exams and study effectively is by reviewing past exam questions and writing out your answers to them. This is particularly effective when there are several years of past exam papers that you can access. When you practise answering the questions, you will get used to what is expected of you in the exam.

Bonus Tip: Don't forget to send your practice answers to your tutors and ask them for feedback. The top-achievers do this all the time and you should too. Make good use of your tutors.

11.   Spot topics well: This is related to the previous point. When you review the past exam papers, you should be able to detect a pattern of the topics that are most frequently examined. Choose the topics that come most often and study them thoroughly. However, be careful with 'spotting'. Make sure you study enough topics so that you can answer the required number of questions in the event that certain popular questions/topics are not repeated in your upcoming exam.

12.   Take care of your body: If you want to achieve good grades and be at your optimum performance, you need to take good care of your body. This should be obvious but it may not be on the forefront of some minds. Studying is stressful, particularly at the tertiary level. To avoid crashing and burning, as stated before, get proper sleep and take breaks often. No one is a robot. You need to eat well and take multivitamins. Eat fruits and vegetables regularly, and dedicate some time to exercise. Drink lots of water. Keep your body and mind healthy.

Bonus tip: If you are feeling overwhelmed, please utilize the counseling services that your school offers. Speak to someone who can help you better handle your issues. Do not bottle it all in; it is not healthy. Get the emotional and psychological assistance that you may need. Again, there is no shame in seeking help.

Those were my twelve tips on how to study effectively. I hope you find them useful and that you implement as many of them as possible to help you succeed at law school.

Chapter 9: Exams

In the last chapter, we covered useful study tips that should help you in your preparation for exams. I hope you find many of them useful and you implement them to prepare yourself for your final exams. Now, in this chapter we will cover what to do immediately before your exam, during your exam and immediately after your exam.

The Day Before

What should you do? By this time, hopefully, you would have covered all the necessary material to prepare yourself for the exam. If you want to succeed and do well in your exams you should not wait until the last minute to study. The day before your exam should be all about revision - your final revision. It should not be the day when you start to learn something new, unless it is just a small topic and you have enough time, energy and mental stamina to take in new material.

Revise your work

On the day before my first exam, I would usually review the entire course at least three times. This would involve me looking over my notes, re-reading important bits of information, and reviewing the past exam questions I would have answered (at least the ones that were marked and reviewed by tutors). I would also review the notes that I would have taken from final revision classes which were conducted by some of the course directors. I would highly advise that you attend those revision classes if possible. Make it your mission to go; the course directors may give you a few tips or a few hints as to which topics may be coming in the exam and which topics to exclude.

However, you should not put all your trust in what they tell you. The course directors may give you information that is vague and easily misinterpreted; they may also tell you that a certain topic would not be examined but then that same topic appears in the exam. That happened for me in first year. Needless to say, the vast majority of the student body was highly displeased when they saw the Civil Practice and Procedure exam paper and it was nothing like what the course director had indicated would be on the exam.

So I would advise that you study as much of the course material as you can. Do not 'spot' too much. You do not want to be surprised in the exam when you do not have enough questions to answer because you didn't study a sufficient number of topics.

Stay calm

You should also try and stay calm. It is very important that you be calm and not panic even if you feel as if you don't know what you are doing, and you feel as if you are studying and you cannot retain any information. I know what this feels like. It is just a temporary feeling. But the more you are stressed about it, the worse you will begin to feel and you will actually believe it. Once you have been attending your classes, doing your revision, answering your past-paper questions, and you understand the topics, you will be fine. The day before the exam is just nerves. You know your work. You need to trust and have confidence in yourself. It is quite normal to be nervous the day before your exams, or very close to your exams. But do not let your nerves defeat you.

Get proper sleep

You should also try to get enough sleep the night before your exam. This is very important. Many people claim that they can study right through the night and into the morning of the exam without sleeping. I do not advise this. Although it may work for some people, it is not a recommended tactic. When you study so hard the night before, you will put extra pressure on yourself which can exhaust you. You may become anxious, cranky and irritable and you might just zone out or fall asleep in the exam room. Of course you would know whether or not this will work for you but again, I would advise not to do so.

Getting proper sleep is very crucial if you want to do well in your exams. You need to have a fresh mind so that you can think clearly. If you are not well-rested, your thought-pattern would be slower and you would become more easily confused. So try and get at least six hours of sleep the night before your exam. That might seem a lot but it is necessary. None of us is a robot. We are human, and humans need rest to recuperate, re-energize and heal.

Prepare your stationery

You should also take this time to prepare all your pens, your pencils, rulers, whatever stationery and items you will need for the exam the next day. Organise your outfit beforehand as well. Make sure that your clothes are ironed and ready so that you would not have to be scrambling and rushing to decide what to wear in the morning, just in case you wake up a bit too late. Also hunt down your exam and student ID cards as well. Secure your IDs together with all of your stationery.

Set an alarm

Additionally, take this time to set an alarm on your clock or your cell phone to ensure that you wake up early. You do not want to be late for your exam. As extra security, you could perhaps have one of your friends give you a call or text in the morning in addition to your phone alarm or your clock alarm to ensure that you wake up on time. Before going to sleep, I would also advise that you say a prayer or two for guidance and wisdom during your exams.

Exam Day

On the day of your exam, you should get up as early as you possibly can. Say a meaningful prayer, a prayer for peace, a sense of calm, and for guidance during the exam. A prayer that God would guide you and that you will stay calm no matter what exam questions appear on the paper. Ensure that you eat a proper breakfast as well. Eat something nutritious that would give you energy during the exam. Eat fruits and nuts. Even if you may be too nervous to eat something fulling, at least drink some juice. Take your vitamins. Drink some water.

Additionally, do some finger exercises for your writing hand, in an effort to reduce cramping in the exam.

Quick review

You can also take this time to do a quick review if you are not too nervous. I know some people do not want to even look at their books or notes on the day of the exam. I normally did my last quick review before I left but I refused to do any more revision once I arrived at the school.

Arrive early

Make sure you get to school early - at least half an hour before the exam starts. Be aware that the fakers will be out in their numbers, looking around trying to find somebody to complain to just to try and bring you down. Avoid them as much as possible. I always avoided people before exams. I did not want to discuss anything to do with the course because I was too nervous. I also did not want to listen to any negativity from anyone to try and upset my mood before the exam.

Do not enter with your cellphone

Ensure that you turn off your cellphone before you go in and make sure that it is not on your person as well. Leave it in your bag outside the exam room. Make sure it is off or in silent mode. This is very important. I remember there was a guy in my class who had forgotten to leave his cellphone in his bag and he had it on him during the exam; apparently it rang. The examiners found out and it was a very big problem for him. I believe he may have been disqualified from writing the exam and he had to go through a set of procedures and stress in order to finally get the administration to allow him to eventually graduate.

Check your stationery

Also take this time to make sure that you have everything you need - your ID card, enough pens, pencils, rulers. I remember for one exam I had forgotten my ruler and I had to borrow one from a very friendly staff member at the office. So make sure that you arrive early enough so that you could borrow anything you need in case you may have forgotten something.

<u>During the Exam</u>

When you enter the exam room, find a seat where you can easily see the clock. This is especially important if you are in a law school that has forbidden students to carry or wear a watch or any electronic device into the exam.

Be aware of the time. You should know how many minutes you need to answer each question, which you should have learned when you practised your past paper exam questions, prior to the exam.

Exam Performance Tips

By now you should be fully aware of what to do in the exam room. If you have reached this far, you would have gone through high school, university and should have a good system for answering your exam questions and doing well in your exams. But nevertheless, here are some tips on what to do during the exam, anyway:

- First things first I would always say a quick prayer for guidance and for a sense of calm and peace during the exam. Breathe. Take a deep breath in, exhale slowly to calm yourself if you tend to be nervous like I was during exams.
- Follow the instructions of the examiners. Do not be rude to any of them.
- Follow the instructions on your exam paper. Answer what you are asked. Make sure you read the paper carefully.

- Select the questions that you are best able to answer and make an attempt to answer all. Even if you run out of time, at least jot down bullet points for the final question if you do not have enough time to answer it fully.
- Before you begin to answer your questions, write down the case names for the questions that you are planning to do. Especially case names that you may forget. Write them down on the side of your question paper or on your scrap paper.
- Jot down your answer plan for guidance. Even if you think that you know it or you know for sure that you are not going to forget, write it down. Quickly outline your structure: the issues, the legal rules, your analysis, the conclusion. Make a few notes on how you are going to answer each question and then start writing.
- Make sure you write as fast as you can and as succinctly as possible. Flex and stretch out your fingers if they cramp up and then keep writing. Ignore the pain. Write through it. Do what you have to do.
- Do not go over your allotted time for each question.
- Stay calm and do not panic.
- Ignore everybody else. Try to shut them out. Just focus on your exam paper and on your ticking time. Ignore the nerd or faker next to you who keeps shooting up their hand to ask for extra paper. I tell you that was so annoying. It used to frustrate me back in my undergraduate years. These persons are just trying to intimidate you. Do not let them rattle you. I later learned that a few of such persons did not even graduate with as high honours as I did. Quantity of answer does not necessarily beat quality of answer in these exams.
- Ensure that you move on to the next question when your time limit for each answer is up. There are only so many marks that you can get for each question. So if

you write a ton of information for one question and a little bit for the other, you are still going to be marked out of the same amount for each question. So do not overdo it.

- When your time is up and the examiner says to stop writing, stop writing at once. Make sure your ID number is filled out on your answer sheets and submit your answer paper.

After your exam, I advise that you go home and take a good rest. Swallow a couple pain killers if your head hurts like mine usually does after exams. Eat something, sleep, rest your brain for a few hours and then get ready for the next exam which may be the next day or the day after that. Use your time wisely to do your final revision for your next exams and you will do well.

Chapter 10: In-Service Training

Earlier on in the year, you will be told about In-Service Training. This is a mandatory ten-week period (it may be more or less weeks depending on your law school) in which students are required to work with a legal entity. This may be with a private attorney, a government institution or a law firm. This training is usually done in the period after exams, normally from June until August.

The purpose of this In-Service Training is supposed to be to help you become acclimatised to the legal environment, the legal working world; it is supposed to help you gain practical experience as opposed to the theoretical knowledge that you would have learned in school. Additionally, it is an opportunity to gain working experience, particularly if you have never had a job before. It is also a great opportunity to network if you are placed in an institution, a firm or chambers.

Apply Early

I would advise that you apply early because you are generally the one responsible for your placement during this period. Apply as early as possible because there are some government institutions like the Attorney General's office that only take a selected number of students and it may be on a first-come, first-served basis. There is also limited space in the well-known law firms. So apply early if you wish to be placed there.

Your Expectation

Depending on where you train, your experience would probably be different from your classmates. For example, what you learn working for an individual attorney would most likely be different from what you learn working in an office in a government institution. Some persons may end up training with criminal law attorneys or family law attorneys, and may be exposed to a plethora of litigation; or they just may end up working in a legal department where they mainly draft documents for the full ten weeks.

So do not expect your experience to be the same as another person's experience. It all depends on where you go and what type of law the person you are assigned to will be practising. If you have never had a job before it is nothing to be scared of. There will be an orientation period - most likely in the first week. You will not be expected to perform exactly as a trained attorney would since you are not yet an attorney; you are just in preparation for becoming one.

If you already know what type of law you are most interested in, I would advise that you sign up with an attorney or an organization that mainly practices that type of law. This would enable you to gain sufficient experience in that type of law to help you determine whether or not you truly enjoy it. Your In-Service Training can be a turning point in your career. It may ultimately help you decide whether or not you intend to pursue law or switch to another, but related career.

During Your In-Service Training

Now, what should you do on your first day, or during your In-Service Training period?

Here are some tips:

- Make sure you go early. You need to make a good impression on your supervisor or whoever you are working for. Arrive to your place of training on time.
- Be professional in whatever you do, especially in your communications. Speak clearly and concisely. Be polite with everyone you come into contact with. This is the time to practice your communication skills, your legal writing skills and your problem-solving ability.
- Learn as much as you can. A lot of the things that you will be doing you would not have learned in law school as yet (depending on where you work, of course).
- Do your research as well. Look for opportunities in which you can research issues or learn things that you did not know before, especially if it will be helpful to you in year two.
- Do not shy away from difficult or challenging issues.
- Volunteer to assist your senior attorney or your supervisor in whatever work they are doing. Do not just sit by and only do the tasks that you have been assigned. Show some extra effort so you can impress your supervisors. You will need them to give you a good report. Depending on your performance, they may keep you in mind and offer you a job when you graduate.
- This is also a good opportunity to network and make connections, especially if you enjoy where you are working and the type of law that they practise.
- Take this opportunity as well to gather as many resources as you can. Collect as many precedents that

you can that would be helpful for you in year two and your legal practice after you graduate.

- Do not forget to ask for help.
- Make sure you carry a notebook and pen with you wherever you go - when you go to court, when you listen in on interviews, when you deal with clients and potential clients. Record everything. Not only is it good for keeping records, but it is also useful as material for your own learning.

Possible Challenges

This may be the first time that some of you would have to interact with members of the public in a legal environment. It may also be the first time that you will be working at all. You may face difficulties adjusting to the new environment but have patience with yourself and learn along the way. It will build your character and make you a stronger, more proficient, well-rounded person who would be much better at your communication skills.

No matter what challenges you face, (e.g. personality clashes with your boss or with fellow students who also work there), do not let them compromise your integrity. Be true to who you are and your principles and whatever you believe in.

There are unfortunately, many unscrupulous, mean and wicked attorneys out there whose sole interests are themselves and making money. Do not allow their negative character traits to rub off on you. They may be excellent in court. They may be excellent at advocacy but that does not mean that they are good role models, or that they possess the qualities that make them a good attorney all around. Do not allow them to compromise who you are, your values and what you stand for. Keep all this in mind while you undertake your In-Service Training so hopefully you will not be as shocked and startled as I was when I found out the true nature of the law profession and the legal fraternity.

A Bit on my Experience

My expectations of what my In-Service Training would have been like turned out to be very far from reality. I am sure my experience was unlike any other. In short, within the very first week of my In-Service Training in June 2015, I was sexually assaulted by my supervisor. When I reported the matter to the partners of the firm, the head of the firm attempted to intimidate me into silence and told me that I had no right to natural justice in her firm. I was shocked beyond belief by her behaviour and pronouncement. I reported my assault to the police, the attorney who assaulted me was eventually charged about a year later, and to this day, the matter is still pending before the Court. But I will elaborate more on this incident in another publication.

Final Tips/ A Word of Precaution

Hopefully, your experience will not be like mine. You can take some precautions to avoid this by doing some thorough research on the attorneys who you may be working with, before you actually apply to be placed with them. Also ensure that you do not work very late, particularly if you are a female; do not be dependent on any attorney to drop you home. Be aware of your surroundings and object immediately to anything that makes you uncomfortable.

If anything similar should happen to you, and you become a victim of a crime, report it at once to your school as well as to the police. Do not allow anyone to intimidate you into silence. Stand up for yourself. You are being trained to be an attorney-at-law and attorneys represent the interests of others. Before you can represent others, you need to be able to represent and stand up for yourself. Do so.

Chapter 11: Aftermath

Your exams are now over and the dreaded waiting period for your exam results is now here. Having to wait several weeks to find out your results can be torturous, but do not fear. Worrying about your marks or your grades will do nothing to change what they will be.

Try to be positive and distract your mind from constantly having to focus on your exam results. Hopefully, your work during your In-Service Training will be enough of a distraction to keep your mind occupied.

Results Day

When the day of the release of your results is finally here, do not freak out. Yes, you will probably be extremely nervous like I was. My stomach was in knots. I could barely concentrate the morning the results were released. I can vividly remember where I was. I was sitting at a desk downstairs in the Legal Aid Clinic (I completed the remaining weeks of my In-Service Training at the Legal Aid Clinic at my law school; I had left the firm for obvious reasons related to my experience, which was mentioned in the previous chapter).

So I was seated there, constantly checking my email to see if the email would come in on time. When it finally did I was so nervous. I did not even want to click on the email to open up the results. I actually hid my eyes after opening the email and peeped through my fingers like a child to see what the grades were. My anxiety was just ridiculous. Nevertheless, I passed all of my exams and I was quite pleased. They were not all A's but hey, I passed and that was the point. The point was to survive law school and I survived my first year.

And I know you will survive as well. I congratulate you in advance for passing all of your exams and surviving your first year at law school.

If You Fail

However, in the unfortunate event that you happen to fail a course or two, do not give up hope. It is not the end of the world. Check your school's regulations to see whether or not they will allow you to re-write your exams later on in August. If so, study hard. See what you did wrong in studying for your exams in May. Request a review of your exam paper and get help from fellow classmates who would have passed or gotten A's in the course that you would have failed. Determine what you did wrong and get the guidance you need in order to correct your mistakes and pass your supplemental exams in August.

Failure is not the end of the world; it is a great teaching tool. It just means that it was not your time to pass. Maybe you misinterpreted a question or two. Now is your chance to do it over and do it better. Everything happens for a reason. A failing grade is not a reflection of who you are as a person or of your true capabilities. Yes, it may be humiliating at first knowing that you have to sit supplemental exams when you have never had to do so before. But you need to think of it from a different perspective. The most brilliant and accomplished people have failed exams or tests or tasks along the way, but it did not make them a failure. In fact, they persevered.

Without failure we would not have learning experiences. We would not know how to do things correctly. We would not have many inventions that we have today. Failing a course and having to repeat the exam or having to repeat the whole year, or even having to drop out of law school, is not the end of the world. In fact, it just may be a pivotal moment in your life to guide you along a new path, along the path that perhaps you were meant to follow.

So if you have to write supplemental exams do not be ashamed. Just be very grateful that you have the opportunity to re-write the exam. Discover what you did wrong the first time around and learn from your mistakes. Do not expect to do the same thing in the same way and expect different results. Do you know what that is? That is the definition of insanity.

Finally...

Once you have completed your In-Service Training, pat yourself on the back and take this time to relax. You would have accomplished a great feat of completing your first year at law school and making it out, hopefully with your sanity intact. Next, it is time to prepare for year two!

About the Author

Giselle Mills is an attorney-at-law who was admitted to the Bar of Trinidad and Tobago in November 2016. She holds a Bachelor of Laws degree from the University of the West Indies and a Legal Education Certificate from the Hugh Wooding Law School. As a student, she found law school to be quite challenging and emotionally-draining. Thus, she decided to share the practical tips she acquired in this book, as a guide for new law students to help them increase their chances of surviving.

Giselle is also the author of the novel *Through It All* which was used by the University of the West Indies as the main text for analysis in the Caribbean Civilisation course for the academic year 2017/2018. Additionally, she is the owner and editor of the new online magazine *Patrice Magazine* which features articles on female empowerment and highlights issues surrounding Caribbean identity.

Follow Giselle on Twitter @ Giselle_Mills or visit her blog: www.gisellemills.com